# Acknowledgements

I have annoyed a lot of people writing this book by sending them stuff or just reading things aloud or asking, "Does this sound okay?" a lot, sorry.

Lots of people have been my muses, my daughter, my wife, my friends, my family, random people I have met, animals!

Here is a quick thank you to a few.

- CBW and EW you are my world, my everything, my lighthouse in the storm.
- Barney you will always be a dickhead.
- My family for the encouragement and reading things even when it was hard.
- JP and EB for being incredibly brave in different ways.
- HH for editing and always challenging me in a clever way.
- MT, LK, IB, AB, JH, RP for listening and reading and praising my work.
- The business staffroom for always asking for more to read.
- HAAB for letting me read to them aloud and practice.
- N and S, and their students for giving me that push and support at the end.
- OB for the incredible artwork. Follow her on @madebylivcreative

One last big thankyou goes to GD. I had only written 3 poems when a friend told me I was good at this poetry malarky, she wasn't bullshitting, she meant it and that meant a lot coming from her. We all have people that will tell us something is good even when it is just okay. That shelf you put up, the meal you cooked, the song you sang. So, when someone with nothing to gain tells you honestly that you are good at something it means a lot. She read all my work first, she made suggestions, she helped me...thank you GD this is all your fault.

A brief explanation of the book, unlike normal poetry where you may wonder regarding the inspiration this book includes my rambling thoughts. You can read the poem and then read my inspiration and then go back to the poem and maybe find alternative insights.

Right... on with the book.

# Contents

# Poem about Me - The beardy bloke

The very first poem in this book is one about me.

The beardy bloke behind the mirror the one only an elite few see.

So, before you read this book you might want to know a few highlights,

Some of my secrets, who I am, what I do, some intriguing insights.

If demographics were poker, the royal flush would be mine.

Middle aged, middle class, white and straight, I am doing simply fine.


I will start with the truth; I have not always been like this.

To write all these poems whilst being holier than thou would be taking the piss,

I was rude and aggressive, loud, a letch, a modern-day cad.

Which is a polite way of saying I was a knob, an arsehole generally bad.

I am not whiter than white, as pure as the driven snow.

In fact, I am sure if you asked people in my past if I were nice, they would certainly say no.

But I am better now, not perfect, but improvements have been made.

The world is a nicer place, and that dickhead part has begun to fade.


I used to drink and classed myself as a high functioning drunk.

I was never late for work, I never ever stunk.

I could hold a conversation 15- or 20-pints in.

The alcohol gave that lovely sheen to my skin.

The drink made me confident, the one who everyone wanted to see,

Oh, so I thought, but the reality was that person wasn't me.

It was fake, a façade, pretend, an illusion, an avatar I created.

He was mean, and hard, and destructive, a person many people hated.

I was tactically sick on many occasions, to ensure that I could keep going.

With spew on my face and snot in my hair, I would arrogantly keep the booze flowing.

I wanted to be the centre of attention, in charge, the lion prowling his lair.

I got whatever I wanted, whoever was in my way, I'd hurt them, I didn't care.

Seemingly destined for the very opposite of heaven

I stopped drinking in 2007.


I am a teacher, I know, it surprises me too,

It's like a proper grown-up job, I wear a shirt and smart shoes.

I teach people, give guidance, and sometimes have tricky conversations.

People call me "Sir", and I pay monthly into a pension.

The bigger surprise is I can do it quite well.

I can read a room, make learning less like hell.

Although interestingly I am not fun, I am all about the rules.

My room is a strict place, I don't suffer fools.

And the students love it, they know where they stand.

We discuss things safely, my room is Switzerland.

I love teaching. I really do. The opportunity to guide a young person,

To give them the tools and opportunities to help them in the race that they run.


I never wanted children, I honestly never did.

Why would I want my perfect life disrupted by some annoying kid?

I was a pretty awesome uncle; you give the kid back and still have fun.

But when I met my amazing my wife, I knew we would soon be dad and mum.

It didn't happen immediately; in fact it took us years.

There was anxiousness, anger, annoyance and quite a lot of tears.

But then it happened we got pregnant; it still seems strange that people say "we",

My wife was doing all the work, the pain, the hurt, she was the one cooking a baby.

I am sure some babies come into the world sweetly like a dream.

Well, ours came in like a rock star, I think everyone involved had a scream.

But now I love being a dad, seriously it is a ball.

It is weird that my best friend is less than 4 feet tall.

I know all dads think it, but I really know it, I know my girl is the best.

She is awesome, she is amazing, she blows my mind, she is better than all the rest.

I get that one day she won't need me anymore and that I will be lame and not cool.

But she is stuck with me, I ain't going anywhere with dad jokes and playing the fool.

She will always be my everything, she holds the key to my soul.

My little girl, my bear, completes me and my wife, makes our family whole.

Why I wrote this book is a simple conversation.

I sometimes struggle with stress, anxiety, and depression.

I tried to journal because it seemed edgy, but I subconsciously ended up lying.

I just ended up reading it back to myself. It was as honest as a couple of pigs flying.

Writing poems helps me get the nonsense out of my head and gives my brain a rest.

I also wanted to try something new. My job is good but "Good is the enemy of the best."

So, I had a crazy idea of voicing my opinion, to look at the world head on, not glazed in pink,

Of authoring a book of poetry that would be accessible to people and make them think.

It is in the reams of possibility; it is not impossible, like me growing back my hair.

Who knows I could become the latest poetry quadzillionaire!

So that is me in a nutshell, I hope you find something in the book that you like,

And in the immortal words of Ant and Dec, watch me drop the mic...sych!

# Poem about Cats - Call your cat Philip

I don't like cats, I think they are annoying, stuck-up little snobs.

If they were turned into humans, you know they'd all be proper knobs.

To them you are a servant, a serf, a member of downstairs staff,

Someone who gets them things. You know they are having a laugh?

We know that they are intelligent, so wise and so serene,

Which means they do things on purpose and that they are basically mean.

If you passed out on the floor dead, they wouldn't shed a tear,

In fact, they would eat your face first, probably starting with an ear.


I get it you like them and that's up to you.

I do admire the way they go somewhere else to poo.

They don't crap in their own garden, they move about and that's fine,

But why have they all chosen that the crap garden should be mine?

Yet another reason for me to think that they are all out to get me,

Also, why ridiculous names like Lunar, Solaris or Fifi?

Maybe that's the reason why all cats are dicks,

Because the stupid names you give them are making them sick.

They want to be called Brian, Philip, Steven or Brad,

Oscar, Jeremiah, Mohammed, Tony even Matt ain't that bad.


So, everyone should call their cat Philip and encourage them to get a job,

Maybe working in a coal mine will stop them from being such a knob.

At least dogs can help society, with blind people or herding sheep,

If a seeing eye cat did exist, it would walk you off something steep.

I know you will all say they are hunters, capturing birds, spiders, and mice,

Well, they only kill for fun they are psychopaths full of vice.

Cats are graceful predators, heightened senses ready for the hunt,

But I don't understand how evolution has turned them into such a... needy,

whingey, fluffy, so and so.

So, enjoy your cat, hear it purr in your lap, and ignore everything that I say,

I am sure your cat is lovely but know deep down inside, it is plotting to kill you some

day.

# Poem about My dog -
# My dog is a dickhead

My dog is such a dickhead, maybe all dogs are.

He'd run absolutely everywhere, be it near or really far.

He could be completely asleep, dreaming of things lying flat on his back.

But by eck he would sprint if he heard you quietly open a snack.

He would lose his freaking mind when someone entered the house.

He'd make a hell of a racket but was as scary as a mouse.

He had a weird innate ability to always try and trip you up.

Standing right in front of you while you hold plates, glasses, or a cup.


My dog is such a dickhead he'd kick off at a T Rex.

I never knew a tiny dog could have such a small man complex.

Put him in a massive field in spring, summer, winter or fall,

And off he would run in the vast, long grass and always come back with a ball.

Attacking that ball like a thing possessed, ripping and tearing that thing in two,

With the added joy the very next day of fluorescent tennis ball poo.

No one tells you how much time you would spend staring at your dog's arse,

Wiping, cleaning, trimming, pulling out plastic, tennis ball fur, and grass.

My dog was such a dickhead but now our little boy has gone.

And for calling him a dickhead, well maybe I was wrong.

But we loved our little dog, he was an original member of the team.

We would run around giggling, laughing playing it really was a scream.

He would lie in my lap insisting that I stroke him for hours and hours,

Yeah, he was a dickhead dog, but that dickhead dog was ours.

We will miss you little pup and your funny made-up voice.

I wouldn't change a single thing even if I had a choice.

# Poem about Alcoholics: Part 1 - Unquenchable thirst

You don't get it, I know you want to, you want to understand.

But you will never know what it's like unless you live it firsthand.

It's strange because it is your mind that betrays you first.

Encouraging your useless skin shell, your body, to create the unquenchable thirst.

Your brain doesn't warn you as the poison invades your vein,

Like the frog slowly boiling in water, it's not logical, it is insane.

Then it's too late and you're broken, your body failing before its time.

Your kidneys are screwed, your liver is done, your stomach lining is turning to slime.


It was at this point the doctor told me I must stop, or I'd die, I had to seriously think.

So, I left the doctor being told I would die, and you know what I did? I had a drink.

I kept drinking because I had it under control. I kept hurting myself more and more,

More often than not I would wake up throwing up blood, curled up on the bathroom floor.

Then one day it happened. I was finished my body failed; I was done.

I remember thinking how sad it would be that my parents would find their dead son,

So, I said a silent prayer for strength and forgiveness for all that I had messed up.

When incredibly I felt a rolling strength flow through me? And I slowly began to get up.

Was it God, was it me, was its drink and drugs that helped me see that I truly had to live?

But on that day, that second, that strength, I knew I would change, I had more to give.


It is not like the movies, in the morning I wasn't dressed by singing birds.

After drinking heavily for 20 years everything was broken and everything hurt.

I was 7 stone overweight; I was smoking and had just lost my major food group.

Seriously, why would I ever stop drinking I was crazy a fricking fruit loop.

So, I drank again, and again and again and I clambered and clawed and tried,

I threw up, I convulsed, I cramped, I was desperate, I screamed, I cried and cried...

But on Christmas day 2007, I tried the hardest I ever had, my new life was ready to begin.

I focused and was getting better when on the 26th, I found a bottle of either vodka or gin.

On the 27th I started again I clambered onto the wagon, and on it I have stayed.

But it's not over, it never will be, I think it is safer to continue; to be afraid.

I think about the cramps and the vomit, the seizures, and the blank spots.

I never take my sobriety for granted and think I am safe because I know that I am not.

# Poem about Alcoholics: Part 2 - I might have a problem

"Oh did you used to be an alcoholic?", is such a ridiculous thing to say.

I **am** an alcoholic, it's my cross to bear, it's with me every day.

Yes, I am in recovery, and I thank my lucky star.

But the temptations and reminders are never very far.

When I see someone homeless, I don't think that could have been me.

It is more that I am terrified that if I slip, it still could be.

People don't understand how easy it is to slip.

The thoughts constantly muttering, filling the bottle drip after drip.

What to do when the bottle threatens to overflow.

Trapped inside your own head with nowhere else to go.

Everything to lose for such insignificant gain.

The fact that tiny gain is attractive is my living shame.


"I was crazy when I was younger, used to drink a bit so I know what it's like."

Droll, these seemingly helpful people with naïve unhelpful insights.

You used to a drink a bit? You haven't got a chuffin' clue.

To wake up so confused, covered in blood, piss, puke or poo.

To be so completely desperate that you would do anything.

Lie, cheat or steal, sell your soul, sell a family ring.

To have one more sip or gulp, you give unto it so freely.

To be lost to this destructive devil, who corrupts your soul completely.

To want to stop but not knowing how because it is all you know.

To want to do better, be better, feel better, to stop feeling so low.


Being a recovering alcoholic means you have to deal with other unique issues.

People explaining how hard they find drinking, sobbing whilst you pass them tissues.

When at a party, people can always track down the alcoholic in the room.

We are always getting cornered by someone whose breath is 50% alcohol by volume.

Patting them on the back or holding their hair as they exorcise themselves at the porcelain shrine.

Still trying to tell me we are the same. Like their weekend binging is a similar problem to mine.

Don't get me wrong, I will always talk about alcoholism when someone really wants to know about that.

But when someone's 3 sheets to the wind, might not be the time for a theological chat.

You may have a problem, you also may not, you may just be normal and like a glass of wine.

You may have a large one at the weekend, enjoy a few shots and that is completely fine.

But if you need help, you should ask, have a conversation even if you don't know what to say.

There are people and groups who can help you Samaritans, Suicide hotline the AA.

# Poem about being a Letch - We're just having a laugh!

Here is a short little anecdote of a time when I was genuinely scared.

A time which made me feel uncomfortable, a time when I was not prepared.

I was working in a bar clearing tables, finding glasses, bottles oh!...weird, look a shoe.

When about 12 mid 20's ladies spotted me on a very drunken shambolic hen do.

They joked and they laughed then one went for my arse, and another one untucked my shirt.

I got kissed on the cheek and my bollocks got groped, but I didn't get physically hurt.

Now some people might think, why is he moaning? Go on! Get in there my son!

Aren't you happy to see those lovely ladies or are you just concealing a gun?

But it was scary and claustrophobic, and it felt out of my control.

They wanted a male stripper, I think and that was not my role.

So, I scrambled and pushed, and forced myself a path.

Then they screamed from behind me "Are you gay? We were just having a laugh!"

I would say that this was a rare occurrence for men, and not many blokes can relate.

But ask the women in your life if they have experienced what I did, and I am sure they all know the date.

A time when they felt isolated by a group of baying hyenas in a pack,

Who were laughing, smiling, and joking but each one of them seemed ready to attack.

But in my situation, I was bigger than the coyotes and cougars around me.

Imagine what it is like when they encompass you and your drowning unable to see,

Needing to push themselves free and escape through the crowd.

Whilst the giggles, whispers and jeers get overly loud.

Doing whatever they can to get free...out...and safe,

"We are just having a laugh!" being shouted in their face.


Letching at girls like baying wolves at a slaughter.

How would you feel if that girl was your daughter?

Does it make it better if you don't know their name?

It makes them invisible and makes you feel less shame.

And if they are invisible, they don't count it won't hurt.

And it isn't anything serious I am just a bit of a flirt.

"I am not touching, it doesn't matter, well I might touch a bit,

It's not my fault she walks around looking so fit!"

I am just having a laugh we all love a bit of banter.

Just using that word makes you sound like a wanker.

Every woman in the world is a sister, aunt, niece or mum.

And not a single one of them wants you trying to smack them on the bum.

It isn't a compliment designed to give them a day of smiles.

Seriously to avoid people like you they would walk a thousand miles.

And no, they didn't dress like that for you, it's up to them where they roam.

If you can't control your reactions in public maybe, you should stay at home.

All the advice tells women, who to avoid, stay in groups and show less skin.

Surely, we can just tell the ones doing the attacking to stop, you know who it is. It's him.

It's him, it's he, it's them, it's they. The boys, the fellas, the geezers, the lads,

Who might be already or one day will be lucky enough to be called dads.


Will you encourage your sons to be just like you, shouting and hollering in the street.

Do you want your daughters to be scared all the time of every man she will meet?

For my little girl I hope she lives in a world where she can be a crazy flamboyant teen.

Where her clothing choices aren't decided by what make her the most unseen.

Where she can go for walks in the dark, safely walking around at night.

And not have to hang around in a group or stay where they have extra lights.

Where she has to politely smile while people holler mean horrible things.

Whilst those derogatory phrases hit her heart and really really sting.

Where she can be who she wants to be, off on adventures she can safely sail.

Currently the only way she can do this is by not being a girl...be a male.

# Poem about Racism - The "but" racist

(Definition someone who tries to hide their racism by precursing with the word but.
For example, I am not a racist.... but....)

There are people in life that you should probably decide to cut.

A lot of us know one, the ones who say, "I am not a racist...but...".

They smile and laugh and touch you on the arm.

The thin veil of politeness that they pass off as charm.

Then they say something jokey with just a hint of hate.

But you decide to let it go because they're family or your mate.

They have always been like it, they're never going to change.

And if we removed the casual racism, they'd have a tiny comedic range.


Who has the responsibility to tell them anyway?

Have we got the right to tell them what to do and what to say?

Surely freedom of speech means they can say and do anything.

But the kicker is they are spreading hate not believing their kids can sing.

Making up excuses about age or what they have seen.

I can't be racist I have friends who are pink, purple and green.

Like that gives them an excuse, a reason, a crazy legitimacy pass.

No nothing gives you an excuse to be a crazy bigoted arse.


Look, the phrase "I don't mean to cause offence",

Doesn't mask your intention or give you a legitimate pretense

To be an arsehole, or overtly mean.

It doesn't make it any better or less of a scene.

They are still a racist, they make peoples skin crawl.

But trying to tell them is like banging your head against a wall.

In answer to the question, "Is it up to you?".

Well, if you aren't going to tell them, then who?


Things have to change, stop saying that's how it has always been done.

The past isn't justification, we are not the centre of the universe, it's the sun.

And just how we learnt that the earth isn't flat.

We now know it's not right to say things like that.

And if you are still itching and saying, "It's my God given right,

To make jokes, have a laugh, it's not serious it's just light."

Well, you are history, a dinosaur scared of the other side of the wall.

And unlike the meteor that killed them I hope that your impact is small.

That your children learnt better than to be filled with hate and with fear.

That they are nice, open and caring not twisted with your insincere sneer.


So, tell them it makes you uncomfortable when they use those hateful words.

It doesn't make us a snowflake or woke, doesn't make us weak or nerds.

It makes us all heroes, no need to feel bad.

We are stronger together a trusted comrad.

It is hate that divides us, it's used to keep us separated.

That isn't how we should live, that isn't how life should be fated.

We should explore with love and compassion in our heart.

We won't let this vocal minority keep us apart.

Keep an ear on what you're saying and the other on your friends,

Because only with people taking notice does this vile cycle end.

# Poem about Teachers 1 - 8 weeks holiday

Swan in at 9 and disappear at 3 everyday.

And we get the bonus of 8 weeks holiday.

All our students love us and are an absolute joy to teach.

With free and open conversation, no one needing to preach.

They debate, they discuss, they positively work through rifts.

And at the end of each academic year, they shower us with gifts.

This might be true on occasion and be every teacher's wish

But the majority of times I must admit this is complete rubbish.


Teaching is bloody hard, and they don't get the thanks they deserve.

If they had a mass teacher walkout, it's the army they would call in as reserve.

My favourite part of Covid was hearing the parents complain.

How hard their little angel is to teach and entertain.

Who can handle a threenager or teenager for 7 hours a day?

Who knows how to keep them busy, which superhero knows what to say?

Well parents you had 1, 2 or 3 and they probably all quite like you.

Now imagine 28 little darlings stuck in a room without a view.


Primary school teachers just do colouring, and babysit a bit.

Are you out of your freaking mind you are clearly talking shit!

These teachers are amazing, they have actual superpowers.

As for being babysitters I bet they want babysitting hours,

10 pounds an hour to look after 1 child.

With 25 in a class, a grand plus a day, would drive those teachers wild.


Secondary school teachers don't exactly get it easy.

Guiding their young people to decisions that would make anyone queasy.

Choose a couple of units at 14 that will help with your future career.

Well, I don't know what I want to be now! Truly it is a very real fear.

Start making them take tests so we know how bright they might be.

But how much a student can remember is the only thing we see.


Colleges and sixth forms have all the stress of exams and real life as well.

They know they're on the final lap, they have heard that ringing bell.

Force them through a bunch of tests, make them jump every hurdle.

Prep them as well as you can for real life, can they complete a Wordle?

And the teachers and lecturers want them to succeed, they really truly do.

Despite the students best efforts to throw it away, we try and get them through.

I have seen teachers sit in the car park before wiping tears away.

Getting their game face on for another stressful day.

Teaching is great but the paperwork attached will kill you.

10, 11, 12 hour days can consume your life, the pressure can slowly fill you.

One piece of work only takes fifteen minutes, so what is the big deal?

Well 100 kids with 2 pieces each, makes 33 hours of marking very real.


Ask a single one of them why they do it, partake in this thankless task;

The vast majority would wonder what a strange thing to ask.

They would smile and say they do it for gifts and the lovely free weekends,

That they do it for the extra holiday, all the free time with family and friends.

They won't tell you the truth the real reason, why they voluntarily enter the lair

It's not complicated. They do it for one simple reason. They do it because they

care.

# Poem about Teachers 2 - Every day is a school day

You probably earn more, have nice holidays, and drive a better car.

But do you honestly change lives at your work and create a living breathing star?

In my job people learn to read, write, and learn to draw their mum and their dad.

In my job we deal with people at their best when they are good and when they are bad.

In my job we help them indiscriminately, everyone deserves better odds.

In my job we help them better themselves, even the ungrateful unfocused sods.


A teacher is something we all had; a teacher is something we need.

A teacher taught you to try new things; a teacher taught you to read.

A teacher helped you to higher education; a teacher taught you to explore.

A teacher helped with difficult discussions, teaching things like beauty or law.

A teacher changed your life, maybe a little, maybe a lot.

A teacher took a chance on you; a teacher gave you a shot.

So be nice to the teachers, who work so hard and don't rock in at 9.

Who help your kids through tricky times and tell them they will be fine.

Be grateful to the teachers who are awesome and don't go home at 3.

Who teach your kids, your nephews, nieces, the whole community.

Be respectful to teaching staff who don't get 8 weeks holiday.

And the last lesson for you to learn is, every day is a school day.

# Poem about Today - The Unfair Sea

It isn't fair, why do these things always happen to me?

Why am I the little boat being thrown about by the unfair sea?

I am having a bad day today, or was it yesterday that was rough?

Why does it seem that every day is getting more and more tough?

It isn't a bad day, it's a shit week, a crap month, an awful year.

And it seems only fair that occasionally I want to shed a tear.

The pile of badness gets higher and higher nothing seems to get better.

This doesn't happen to anyone else; it seems like a personal vendetta.


Firstly, the gods aren't out to get you, they have more important things to do.

They have pyramids to build, henges to make, dinosaurs to pull out of primordial goo.

Human beings are programmed to remember the bad things, so we survive.

It's basic evolution because if something is bad, we should avoid it and stay alive.

If you look at the world and only see the dark, then you miss out on what's right.

If you only think about a half empty glass, you will fail to see the light.

We are all willing to accept that we have good days and bad.

But we scream when it goes wrong but when it goes right, why aren't we glad?


Clouds have silver linings; rainbows appear after storms.

After the darkness of the blackest night, we always have the dawn.

I try to regret nothing about yesterday or about the day before.

It made me who I am today, it made me able to soar.

I try my hardest to be thankful because good happens every day.

It is around us in our actions, what we do and what we say.

So, if it feels bleak, take a breath, this too shall pass.

Think of the joy in the world, share a smile or a laugh.


We don't need to make grand gestures to improve someone's day.

It can be a smile, a conversation, a wave, a simple explanation, a "hey!"

We are able to make a difference to the people all around us.

You can make little differences; you don't have to shout or make a fuss.

Kindness and niceness can be contagious addictions we should all embrace.

They are medals of honour, badges of pride, to wear upon our face.

If it's a good day for you, share the love, help others, go the extra mile.

You don't know when you might feel blue and need someone to make you smile.

# Poem about Mums -
# The impossible job

(Definition: like a dad but they don't have to ask for permission first and they know where everything is.)

Mums can be mums and mums can be dads,

They can be aunts and uncles, grandmas and grandads.

It takes a village to raise a child and help with the relief.

But never forget that the mum is the boss the big chief.

It is an impossible job with not enough praise.

If it was advertised in the private sector, they would get a weekly raise.

They will never drop you and never let you go.

They will still be your mum forever through the highs and if you're low.

You may argue with each other, say mean and awful things.

But I promise they love you completely they are your angel without wings.


A mums reaction time is remarkable a truly incredible thing.

Like a featherweight exchanging punches lightning fast inside the ring.

A mum can be snoozing completely, dead to the world tick tock, tick tock then

tick.

But with a whinny or whelp from their child, they will be through two doors using bowls or their hands to catch sick.

As a dad I am still in the land of nod, my foot hasn't even hit the floor.

A mum is holding a slowly filling bowl and I am drowsily heading to the door.

I make light, but I've seen the desperation of trying anything when your kid is poorly or upset.

And having to rely on something hateful and awful like the vapid world of Mumsnet.

Double guessing every decision because they want the best for their kid.

The truth is everyone is guessing or just explaining the different things they did.


A Mum is a gift, a blessing, a saint.

She is as strong as an ox, she is your best mate.

She is the first to praise you, the first to criticize.

They speak the truth and have caring eyes.

They give the best snuggles and they will hold you close to their heart.

A mum becomes complete with a child they are the missing part.

A mums love for her child is a solid physical thing.

It connects them forever like an unbreakable string.

Never mind the distance, the connection will always be there.

They bandaged your knee; they brushed and combed your hair.


You are older now and probably have an appreciation for the role.

For the majority of us, our mums protected us, bandaged our bodies, saved our souls.

If you are blessed and your mother/mummy/mama/mum is still around,

Give them a call, say you love them, they will never tire of that sound.

And if you're a mum and you're reading this, you are doing a great job,

Even though your kid can be frustrating, confusing, a bit of a knob.

Remember, It is okay not to like them every minute of the day,

Because whatever happens you love them completely, come what may.

This is a thank you to the mums that astound me that I am blessed to know,

In fact it's to all the mums who need a reminder that you were the ones that

helped us grow.

# A Poem about love -
# Love is spiffing

Love is incredible, love is unseen.

Love is a sentiment It is, "your somewhere that's green".

It can hurt, make you cry, make you laugh, make you sigh,

Make you giggle, make you sob, make you crazy, quit your job.

To leave the big smoke and fly across the earth

Because you think, you believe, no, you know what it's worth.


Your heart can skip, it can jump, it can flutter.

It can make someone confident suddenly develop a stutter.

A chatty person becomes mute, the shy one a talker.

You think about them constantly, no nicely, not like a stalker!

Your heart can race, and your breath be stolen away.

After years and years, it can still feel like the first day.

The first moment, the first second that fraction of time.

When you saw them completely and thought "that one's mine".

You see the real them the one that no one else knows.

The one without makeup wearing threadbare old clothes.

A love that's so massive high, deep, long and wide.

You can fart in the open now, you don't have to hide.


They can be hugely inappropriate, they snort when they laugh.

They're your wingman your partner, you forge the same path.

You are stronger together much weaker apart.

You are each other's completely, one mind and one heart.

When you feel happy, excited, depressed, mad, or blue.

Look at the sky wherever you are and know it is for the two of you.


Love can be fleeting and last through the ages.

It will never be long enough, never enough pages.

So go on adventures, forget the bad people you met.

Enjoy overpriced meals and every terrible boxset.

You survived through a plague, who else can say that?

Well, it was a global pandemic so everyone as a matter of fact!


In closing loves spiffing, it's splendid it's fab.

So, if you feel it with someone just reach out and grab.

If you have someone special, congratulations, you won.

Because if love was a race, make sure that you run.

And if a sporting analogy doesn't' work, doesn't fit.

Get the one you love, some cake, a movie, hold their hand and just sit.

# Poem about My girl - Number 1 guy

I can't find your parting as well as your mum.

And I had to be shown how to wipe your bum.

One day we will be brave and attempt a plait.

I will almost definitely make a mess of that.

Everyone can tell when your dad dresses you.

With spots mixed with stripes, one sandal, one shoe.

Everything you want I promise I'll try.

Because above all I was your number 1 guy.


I held you first, yep, that was me.

Been covered in puke, poop, bogey and wee.

Suggested things that were dangerous and silly.

Had to explain why you don't have a willy.

And that won't be our last difficult chat.

I am absolutely certain, and terrified by that.

You are already asking where, who, what and why?

And I will always answer as your number 1 guy.


Everyone told me this job would be tough.

Honestly climbing Mount Everest wouldn't have been as rough.

At the beginning your guessing, "What does this little girl think?"

Am I doing the right thing hosing her down in the sink?

Is she full or hungry, too hot or too cold?

Why does she cry when I pick her up for a hold?

But you know what we did it and came through the muddle.

And remember there not "holds" they're snuggles and cuddles.

Yes, I struggled and stressed, internally screamed, had a cry.

But it was all worth it to be your number 1 guy.


And now you're much bigger and running about.

Climbing and jumping and by eck, can you shout?

You run and you scoot and you climb everything.

You'll chat with anyone, you love to dance, love to sing.

You amaze me each day, you can do anything it seems.

Your mum, me and you we are the best team.

Your hair is so long now it is beginning to curl.

You're not a baby or toddler you're a big little girl.

I still can't find your parting, you look at me and sigh.

"Doesn't matter daddy I love you", yup, I'm her number 1 guy.

# Poem about Men - Yellow Cress

Weeing standing up is not an easy thing to do.

Not the direction you thought I would take on this poem I know.

But being a woman is like super, super tough.

So, moaning about being a man seems a little rough.

So, I am not going to belittle things and think woe is me.

I will talk about the real important stuff like going for a wee.

Women just think it is pissing in a ceramic bowl.

It's not, it's pressure, angles, speed like navigating a black hole.

When you line it up perfectly, but it comes out its wonky.

Like a drunken version of pin the tail on the donkey.


We understand that it is frustrating when we get the toilet seat wet.

When you get that pungent aroma coming from a yellowish carpet.

Having carpet in a toilet is a terrible idea we must confess.

It's so soggy if you chucked some seed on it, you'd get stinky yellow cress.

With morning glory its worse like shooting in the dark.

In that circumstance, it's almost impossible to hit the perfect mark.

The annoyance of 95% going exactly where you require.

Whilst the last 5% isn't even in the same range of fire.

Holding the lid up, levering pant elastic and poking it through a fly.

Is it really any surprise that we can't keep the toilet seat dry?


And now I have mentioned this most important of topics, there is just one little thing left to discuss.

It is the fact that men are shit at sharing our true emotions, we don't like to cause a fuss.

I apologize that I have hidden my true intentions, but this poem it isn't really about wee.

I want to mention something important, a problem not tangible, something we can't see.

Suicide is a problem; it's killing men faster than cancer and it can be prevented by having a chat.

So, talk to a mate, see how they are, your mates are all dickheads, but they are probably worth that.

Ask how they are and then ask them again, tell them It's okay to talk me.

It's quite important to do these things but maybe not as important as the difficulty of the standing wee.

One last word on pissing and this last part might make you frown.

If you really can't handle not peeing on the seat, then seriously sit the chuff down!

# Poem about Black dog -
# My dog is different

Black dogs have been used throughout history, throughout time.

As a metaphor, an example, a handy little rhyme.

To depict addiction, anxiety, anger, or stress.

To try and explain why your head is a mess.

Now my dog is different, but I know that it's mine.

They don't have to be the same, surely that's fine.


Yeah, my head is a mess but probably different from yours.

But my dog gets in there ripping with its' teeth and its' claws.

It can make me think things that I don't want to think.

Combining issues and stresses with link after link.

Even good things can be problems when you're alone in your head..

Lying in the darkness sinking deeper into your bed.

Thinking about death but not wanting to die.

Going for long walks and needing to cry.

Knowing what hurts you and trying to stay afloat.

Creating battlements and towers, hell, build a psychic moat.

But those dogs can be so tricky searching for gaps high and low.

They will build a mental dinghy and across the moat they'll row.


As a kid no one told you your life would be so hard.

You always assumed that you'd be able to predict every card.

That life would be simple and adulting would be easy.

When, in reality just checking emails can make you queasy.

Sometimes it feels like you are stuck in a rut.

And that dog comes along just to kick your butt.


Find a way of venting to keep the black dog out.

Of screaming and clawing an internal shout.

It is important to find a way of relieving the pressure.

Something physical, intelligent, something strict or just leisure.

Whatever it is, just do it, it will help you.

I found something, it helped me, it can help you too.

# Poem about Cancer - Nuff said

Cancer you are a dick.

This doesn't rhyme, it isn't a poem in the way that I write poems, I didn't take my time, it is a rant of little consequence.

Cancer doesn't deserve a place in this book, cancer can fuck right off, it has taken too much, too many.

It has affected us all, no one hasn't been touched by it, it tried to take my sister, my dad, my friends, and those too young, too bright, too shiny and too much to be lost.

So, I repeat cancer can fuck right off, I will not give it a place or any more thought. I don't like to use the word hate because hate requires energy and I refuse to give cancer anything at all. I hold it in disdain.

It is nothing, it is a petty, putrid vile thing that doesn't get a poem in my book. It doesn't get that privilege...cancer, you are a dick.

# Poem about White Britishness - Mongrel Nation

A friend asked me about white Britishness, why we don't celebrate it?

Well, the answer is simple white Britishness does not exist.

Don't get me wrong I am incredibly proud to be British.

We are amazing, a smorgasbord, a buffet kind of dish.

We lent, borrowed, and stole from other nations, it made us who we are.

We travelled all around the world pinching stuff near and far.


"But Britain is white, and I am white, I wanna shout about my origins."

If you wanna do that, do a DNA test. Look at the Gaelics, the Swedes, the Fins.

We are a bastard nation, a bunch of mongrels, a classic Heinz 57 variety.

Our language has a smattering of everything, Hindi gave us the word trigonometry.

What about the other people who are different, and they want to know about their past.

Why are they allowed to be noisy, have street parties, eat weird things, or fast.

That is different, unlike some people who want to paint their country with a colour.

They want to colour in the country with flavour and make our multiculturalism fuller.


So black celebrate black; white do white, all the colours explore your background.

Each look into your paths and celebrate the things that you've found.

The reason to explore your heritage is to see where your ancestors thrived.

It's where your past was born and where it has hopefully, survived.

Don't think about your bit as separate, think about how they all just blend.

How with the mixture of colour and culture we could bring the racism to an end.

I know it feel like racism is a fight that you just cannot win.

A start would be stop judging people because they have different colour skin.


Absolutely celebrate Britishness I am British, and I am proud.

Shouting about white Britishness seems like being loud for the sake of being loud.

White Britishness is not a thing, we don't share a heritage in that way.

We are however all British and you know what, that's okay.

So, wave a flag, wear a shirt, paint flags upon your face.

It doesn't matter what freaking colour we are, we celebrate that we live in the same place.

# Poem about Annoyance - Legitimate slowness

When I was 14 I had a job tidying up supermarket trolleys.

Back then it was easy, they would be found in the bays, not too many wallies?

But now people have gone mad a level of anarchy that I don't think is okay.

To abandon a trolley and not take it back to the clearly allocated bay.

When a trolley ends up in a canal I can kind of understand.

Teenagers think it is funny and rebellion happens, I've seen it firsthand.

When an adult does it, it's laziness, trying to save time, cause they know better.

Seriously, the 10 second you saved what are you doing writing a letter?

Seriously, what kind of a sociopath doesn't return a trolley?

That leaves it in a parking space and clearly isn't sorry.

Its someone else's job, someone else will do it.

That kind of introverted thinking makes you such a tit.


No truer way to prove you are an absolute dick.

Then not helping the world and using your indicating stick.

It is niceness, it's politeness, to show you are moving into that space.

For God's sake you are not taking part in a real-life death race.

You aren't Mad Max in a desperate search for water.

Why are you trying to run over my wife, mum, or daughter?

On the flip side of that, still making me angry and scoff.

Is when those complete morons can't turn the indicator off.

How far left are you intending to go?

And if you aren't taking this left then why are you going so slow?

Can you not hear the annoying tick tick tick tick?

Turn the bloody thing off then, you annoying prick.


I have thought for a while that pavements should have lanes.

You know for the slow dawdlers, the ones that drive me insane.

Don't get me wrong, I don't mean legitimate slowness like a limp or a pram.

I mean the meanderers with no direction who gambol about like lambs.

Walking about this way and that, over here and over there.

Chatting on their phone, listening to music, or flicking their hair.

How do people not know that someone's trying to get past?

Get out of my blooming way slowpoke, move if you are not that fast.

People should pay more attention of what's happening, they really should take note.

At the next election screw the Prime Minister, this is the issue on what we should vote.

The solution is simple, have two lanes on the pavement all the way along.

One for the people who walk normally and another for the people who are wrong.

This is a poem that I will probably revisit because things will continue to frustrate.

If I tried to include absolutely everything, I would be typing until very late.

So, in later adaptations I will include other things like courgettes and gone off milk.

Overpriced snacks, electric scooters, fakeon and things that are soft like silk.

The fact I don't like really soft things is a story for another day.

But remember one thing, when you're walking, get out of my chuffing way.

# Poem about Age - Rolling stone

When you are young you want to be old

You don't listen to any of the advice that you're told

You try new things, do what other kids are doing and try and be a little bit cool

When you want to start going a little crazy, you want to start playing the fool

You want to push boundaries get another feather in your cap

You don't realize that it's true when they say growing up is a trap

We are so desperate to grow up but how do we know that we are grown

At what point do we start to enjoy a good grumble and a moan

At what point are you an adult doing all the adulting things

Getting to enjoy yourself, going out buying fancy rings


Well, I am old, and I think they lied being a grown up is quite tricky

My back hurts, my eyes are knacked and I kinda want to chuck a sicky

I make noises when I sit, I make noises when I stand

I have to crack my knuckles, or I can't use my hand

I try to get better and try to get fit, use apps to check my paces

In all honesty I get out of breath just trying to tie my shoelaces

I know that I am old because at the cinema I don't order anything large or fizzy

I order a medium latte, don't get anything too big or I will have to get up for a wee

The amount of film I miss because I have to nip to the loo

Walking in front of movie goers and annoying people like you


I have lost all my hair, got two inches on my waist and I have glasses to improve my sight

It annoys me that people drive too fast or too slow, all I know is that my speed is just right

I moan about music on the radio can't make out the words that they say

Truthfully, the worst music of the 90s is better than most of the crap spewed today

I know it sounds cliché, but stuff was better when we were younger

A simple meal at Mr Wimpy on proper plates was enough to quench our hunger

We played out at night and only went home when it got really really dark

Our favourite place was under a bridge, down the canal or messing about the park

We only had three channels, but we had bat shit Tv and crazy crazy cartoons

Like Pob, Supergran, rentaghost, Finder's keepers, Fun house, and Button Moon


I am old and I might talk about the weather and how life could be a bit crappier

But the weird thing, and honestly, I'm not joking I really really couldn't be happier

I think the kids might be right getting older can be great

But not because of parties or craziness or even staying up late

Getting older may mean responsibilities but it also means you don't have to give a toss

I am older, not wiser, not rich but not a miser like the cool rolling stone that has no moss.

I can do what I want to go to bed when I want...which is usually about half past nine

I have money and can buy what I want although it's bills rather than cheese or wine

It may seem mundane to the crazy youths of today, but I really am honestly happy

So, enjoy what you have be it young, middlin or old otherwise you will always feel crappy

# Poem about Pressure - Saggy bits and flappy bits

Do this, do that, go here, go there.

Look like this or that, smart face cute hair.

Buy a house, buy a car, go on holiday near or far.

Can't afford it, just lease it, don't lower the bar.

The world has expectations of who you should be.

The person, the reflection, the one you want people to see.


You need a tiny waist but a bust and a massive arse.

This body shape ideal is a joke, a fucking farce.

Young men need to be ripped; how can a six pack not be enough?

You need an eight pack that's silky smooth, don't be real don't be rough.

An unwritten list of criteria that is how others can judge and rate someone.

How can a constantly changing checklist be a fair thing to assess anyone?

Although the unwritten nature of this criteria seems to be becoming more

transparent every day.

People are being called out for ridiculous things, what gives a stranger the right to have a say?


People critique everything, tangible stuff like body shape, size, girth and money.

Even the intangible elements like body count, followers, how often you're tasting honey.

Our online and physical life is continuing to get tougher and tougher.

As the expectations of reality and social media continue to be rougher.

Whatsapp it, gram it, do a freaking TikTok.

Get your brows on fleek, get your look on lock.

And we bow and we scrape because we want people to like us.

We giggle along, we smile, we laugh, we don't want to cause a fuss.


You would think that this pressure was transient like puberty.

But the pressure still exists at sixty, fifty, forty, thirty.

Lack of hairline, bigger belly, yellow teeth, whole body sprouting hair.

Saggy bits and flappy bits and expectations that just aren't fair.

I get it, stay healthy and fit, that is a sensible thing to do.

But a little spread over 30 or 40 should be okay for me and you.

I click on social media; everyone is pretty and thin and great.

My logical mind is telling me ignore them I know they are fake.

The pressure is real though they do make me feel insecure.

They make me question things they make me feel unsure.


How about I don't judge you and you don't judge me.

We'll just be nice to each other and see what we will see.

We can be civil and polite; we all could just be nice.

People could comment on an outfit without having to Google the price.

People could eat what they like without photos just cause it's yummy.

I can put on a little weight without someone patting my tummy.

Go out with messy hair, unshaven and no make up on.

Wear comfy clothes for comfy clothes sake, why is that so wrong?

Don't put so much pressure on each other, just relax a little for chuffs sake.

The most important thing though, out of everything, is give yourself a break.

# Poem about Manly men - Keeping it up

There are different types of men those who are wolves and those who are pups.

These men who are strong and dependable and can always get it up.

They don't need assistance or help; they can do it all on their own.

The manliest of man, the don, the daddy, they all deserve a throne.

It's amazing how solid it looks, straight, strong, and erect.

Even from a distance it has that perfect, sculpted renaissance effect.

They make the rest of us feel weak, insignificant and make us cry.

We all bow down at the altars of the kings of DIY.


It can be flat pack, bespoke, outside or in.

There is nothing they can't do like a chameleon changing its skin.

They have the latest Pinterest idea embedded in their home.

Like the hanging gardens of Babylon or the coliseum pillars in Rome.

They always have a project on and even worse they always finish.

Even the ad hoc projects are brilliant and not a little bit rubbish.

The colour palette in their home is tasteful and well thought out.

And frustratingly they are modest, and they don't like to shout.

They say things like, "It's easy you could make something like this too."

You are trying to be nice dude, but if I tried that it would look like poo.


Maybe it is because they have all the right kit, and they know what each tool is called.

All my tools have been inherited from family. I have a toolbox, but no one is fooled.

What if DIYers are just more patient and are able to stay cool and chill.

What if DIYers really enjoy it and for them it is exciting and a real thrill.

They watch a YouTube video once and bam they are able to do it.

I could plan for a thousand years, and it would still look like shit.

I can plan and design, sketch and draw, envisage what I want to create.

I tried to do it, but I can't do it, when I was younger it became a disdain and hate.

Then I realized not everyone is good with their hands, we can't all mend, reuse or make.

You don't have to feel bad about it, have a cuppa and call a professional for chuffs sake.

# Poem about Violence 1 - Washed in the rain

I saw something bad happen, it didn't happen to me.

But now when I close my eyes it seems to be all I see.

It is like the graphic images can't be deleted or filed away.

Like they do the rounds for a little bit then appear back in my in-tray.

I am not sure how to process it, not sure how I am supposed to think.

It keeps wanting to stick around like beard trimmings circling a sink.

I am sure it will dissipate like blood washed in the rain.

Let me try and tell you what happened, let me try and explain.


I saw a man attacked with a machete; it is something I will never unsee.

I know that it is logged and remembered; it is something stuck inside me.

It is the most brutal and graphic thing I have ever seen in my life.

The utter hatred that was used and delivered at the end of that knife.

I have seen violence, hatred, and blood. I am not whiter than white.

I have thrown the first punch; been beaten up, I have been in a couple of fights.

But this wasn't a fight, a punch up or a scuffle. It was an attack, an assassination attempt.

The attacker was blinded by anger and hate, and the victim was held in utter contempt.


I am struggling to process it; it continues to rattle around.

It sometimes makes me feel topsy; I can't find the ground.

People ask how I am? What I saw? They question me about it.

Then immediately reverse because no one wants to hear the gritty bits.

I don't feel guilty as I helped the victim and he is recovering, he is alive.

I didn't do much, just held things and raised his legs; maybe I helped him to survive.

I don't feel fear as the attacker was caught and will end up in jail.

I do feel angry, but I am always a little angry because respect for life is so frail.

I am lucky as I have family and friends who will listen and keep me straight.

If you see something, talk to people, reflect, do not allow yourself to be saturated with hate.

That is what I will do, I will process it slowly and my mind will clear.

I will not allow the hate of the world make me be governed by fear.

# Poem about Violence 2 - Pushing buttons

When someone disagrees with you on something you can usually have a discussion.

But when someone is belligerent, so angry or stupid the chat can become a concussion.

The problem with belligerent people they are sheer bloody minded.

Everything is so clear to them the argument is completely one-sided.

They believe something completely like hating someone or something.

And hatred can be aimed at stuff like sexuality, religion or skin.

I've seen fights start for ridiculous reasons if anger goes unchecked.

Someone looked at you strange or some ludicrous perceived disrespect.

Drugs, alcohol, peer pressure, size and overinflated ego that believes so fully.

That takes rational human beings and turns them into domineering bullies.


People try and push your buttons by calling you names or your sister a whore.

Don't take the bait, walk away, your sister, mum, girlfriend prefer you alive and free more.

One punch can be the domino that destroys a bunch of lives.

You don't know whose skull is thin or who is carrying knives.

I am not a devout pacifist; I am not sitting on the fence.

But I do think the last resort is only when you should consider violence.

So, walk away, run away if you have to, just get away from the issue.

Why do we have to "man up", why in movies is it that that they teach you?

Is it cowardice or intelligence that makes us turn the other cheek?

Why is the perception of someone who won't fight as someone mild or meek?


I think some people are wrong and other people are right.

I believe some people think something so deeply the only option is to fight.

The issue is for you to be right then someone else has to be wrong.

And the further issue with violence is that it can be someone's swan song.

In the first verse I talked about belligerence and in the second it is walking away.

In the verse I am a little confused I don't know what else to say.

Violence is bad, hurting people is bad, surely we all understand that.

It won't make things better taking revenge at the end of a blade or a bat.

Staying alive is the priority, learning is the key, just grow, survive, and evolve.

Through communication, discussion and learning there isn't a problem you cannot solve.

# Poem about Unicorns - Their mojo doesn't fail

I asked my little girl, "When you are older what do you want to be?"

She shouted "unicorn" without missing a beat.

I did try to point out that unicorn isn't really a proper job.

When I mentioned this, she looked at me like I was a proper knob.

I agreed anything is possible and that maybe I was wrong.

I would do a little research into poems, books, and songs.


A unicorn is a mythical beast, a wondrous and amazing thing.

In all depictions they are perfect, even able to dance and sing.

They are sparkly and shiny, beautiful, and clean.

You know what they look like even though they are never seen.

With a rainbow mane and a beautiful flowing rainbow tail.

With a healthy coat they look banging, their mojo doesn't fail.

The stories about unicorns are awesome and great to tell.

They are so impressive, I bet their trumps don't even smell.

They are tirelessly chilled, effortlessly awesome, and never seem to get tired.

They would be employee of the month every time and never ever get fired.

They make friends so easily; let anyone join their team.

They are loyal and go together so well like strawberries and cream.


Unicorns would load the dishwasher, crack a window when they go for a poo.

They would tell you that you look fabulous, they would change the paper in the loo.

They would remember every birthday, anniversary and celebrate it with passion.

They will embrace every style but just being themselves is the best fashion.

They would never steal the blankets or hog the remote control.

They would mean it when they asked if you are okay and help you out of a hole.


All unicorns are individual and beautiful inside and out.

We should all strive to be unicorns and give that lifestyle a shout.

Be rainbow colored and glittery, fabulous in every way.

Unicorns never get flustered they always know what to say.

Maybe she is right, and I will join her crazy unicorn cult.

And I will also be a unicorn when I become an adult.

# Poem about New parents - Avalanche of crap

I love having a kid, I really truly do. It is incredible an absolute gift.

If I have a hard day, just seeing her makes my heart skip a beat, and lift.

When I was preparing for the birth, I read a book so I would be ready for it.

After the birth, realized none of the important stuff was mentioned and the rest was absolute bullshit.


Getting in practice, putting a baby grow on a doll, swaddle it and pop on a little hat.

You want some realistic practice, keep the baby grow but swap the doll for a feral cat.

Babies are a cross between a sumo wrestler and Houdini, that has a strange vendetta against you.

and the fact that you must be faster than a pit crew before the next wee or poo.

Seriously no one told me how much time I would spend talking about poo.

Consistency, colour, frequency the questions are continuously on a loop.

New parents discuss poonamis, avalanches of crap and the terrible stink.

Wait until they move onto solids, now that is a smell that will make you think.


Everyone knows you won't sleep, and we all accept that it will be fine.

Although 3am with a wailing child can make for a very lonely time.

Rubbing backs, patting bottoms, stroking hands as you quietly shush and weep.

Praying to gods, making deals with the devil, please let my baby sleep.


No one tells you that teething problems goes on for chuffing years.

And that it has a million symptoms like nappy rash, vomiting and loads of tears.

When you mention this to another parent, they giggle like it is a secret little trick.

You could have let me know, you dickhead, yeah you, you sanctimonious prick.


But through all of this you slowly realize that all of that stuff doesn't matter.

That your perceptions of being a parent should be thrown away and shatter.

That although it is difficult, tough, exhausting, physically and mentally you are wrecked,

It's also wonderful and beautiful and incredible and your individual kind of perfect.


Little miracles begin to happen that will totally envelope your heart.

You realize that being a parent is miraculous and the annoyance a smaller part.

When they first grasp your finger, or smile, laugh, speak and walk.

It's beautiful when they chunter, they babble, say your name, and start to talk.


It is you they want when they are scared or excited when they want to share something new.

They like other people and enjoy being around them, but their favourite person is you.

When they hold your hand or sit with you, they feel safe and completely at peace.

They babble and tell you the craziest things you're their BFF, you're their release.


So yes, it is hard and scary, depressing and angering at times.

But bear with it because I promise you are in for a big surprise.

Those little yous are perfectly perfect, they complete your family.

So, don't be hard on yourself, you're doing great they love you unconditionally.

# Why I wrote each of the poems

## ~~Why did I write it.~~ -
## My rambling thoughts

# 1. Poem about me- The Beardy bloke

This seems to be a waste of paper because the poem itself explains why I wrote this book. Although I will explain what my original motivation was, originally it was a book for men. Men are rubbish. We are. So this book is here so to make people question things and make people think. Then it evolved into more about me, who I am and what I think, where I have been and what I have done. The poems became an outlet for me to vent, to process, to function. I write and I release, and a surprising side effect is that people seem to enjoy my blabberings my chuntering, my poems. Everything I write is based on my opinions and are based on truth and did really happen.

Then it evolved again, it was my mum that suggested that it could be a book of two halves, that at the back I could include details about why I wrote each poem, where I was in my life, in the world. What motivations were encouraging me to write each of them what anecdotes can I attach to explain my opinions and mindset. Well thanks mum what a ridiculous idea that was, it has taken me much longer to write these little paragraphs than the actual poems.

Anything else you need to know? I love rugby (watching not playing, I would break), I love cooking, the best drink in the world is ice cold Coca Cola in a glass bottle. I am not built for the heat and prefer a hoodie then a speedo. I have several mantras in my life that help to guide me, "It's always nice to be nice." and "I can't do it yet." But I only have one in a frame on my desk, "Every sinner has a future, every saint has a past." I truly believe in second chances and that we all deserve to be saved if we want to be.

I have an Instagram account, thebeardybloke110, where I release content on the 27th of each month (if you have read the book, you know why that is important), don't expect or ask for more content, I like to be consistent.

Enjoy my little poetry book, allow it to make you laugh, make you cry, to question things and wonder why.

Tell your friends how awesome it is but don't lend them a copy and encourage them to buy.

## 2. Poem about Cat- Call your cat Philip

I don't like cats, when I was a kid we had a cat called Whisper and I hated her. She was completely black and would sit on top of the video player (look it up) for warmth. She was so dark you couldn't see her so when you went to get a tape out or pop a tape in the little git would scratch you. If that wasn't a good enough reason, he once left a dead mouse on my collection of Asterix books (again look it up) not just a single, peaceful looking restful body she chuffing vivisected that blooming thing all over them, all of which gives me good reason to hate cats.

The other thing that drives me mad about them is they know who doesn't want to pet them. I am not the biggest fan of physical contact, I believe that hugs should be saved for certain people and special occasions, cats are floosies. Throwing themselves at people who aren't interested like a drunken person at quarter to two in the morning at a nightclub, rubbing themselves against someone who is clearly not interested.

However, I worked with a bloke called Matt and he loves his cats...too much. His cats had a robot litter tray, automatic feeding stations, he wanted to buy one of those cats' carrying back packs with a window in it! He was leaving where we worked and to be honest, I liked him, he was a nice guy and I wanted to give him a nice leaving present, so I wrote it for him and his unnatural love for his cats.

## 3. Poem about Dog- My dogs a dickhead

When my sister went to university my parents replaced her with a dog (brutal I know but it gets worse), when I went to drama school they replaced me with a plant, I am hoping these gifts didn't reflect our personalities... the plant lived longer than the dog...just saying. I ramble but let me be clear. Cats bad. Dogs awesome. So why I wrote this isn't just my preference of dogs being best but our dog Barney, he really is a dickhead, but he is ours. He was diagnosed with prostate cancer in April 2022, and we were told in no uncertain terms he had 6 months to a year. We are currently in November, and he is being as belligerent as ever holding on, loving going for walks and eating all he can but he is walking slower, sleeping more and generally more in an arse. He hasn't got long, and I will be sad when he leaves but he had a good life and for now he is still trying to trip me up and still devouring tennis balls.

My dog just died, and I was right I am sad. I have always had dogs, but this is the first time I have had to be the adult. I have had to book the euthanasia, take him, hold him and watch him fall asleep...absolutely fucking broke me.

I wrote this poem about our dog because he was an incredibly important member of our family, he was our first baby, he was an integral family member. He will be missed; he will leave a hole in many ways no more so than the weird voice we invented for him. Over the years my wife and I created a strange personality and voice for our dog. A weird miserable northerner. The way it works is, if I come in the room and ask Barney "How's it going?", my wife would respond in the dogs' voice, really really made me laugh...in fact there is a good chance the ghost of Barney will pipe up soon with "Still here knobber you can't get rid of me!"

# 4. Poem about alcohol 1-Insatiable thirst

My name is Mark and I am an alcoholic, I didn't used to be an alcoholic, I am a recovering alcoholic, I am not a drunk, drunks get hammered alcoholics go to meetings. It isn't a badge of honor or me proving my worth or showing how interesting I am, it is something dark putrid and rotting inside of me. I still pause in shops, I still steady myself when I walk into restaurants and bars, I dream about it so vividly I wake up scared as I am phantom hungover. It is a battle every moment and it is a battle I intend to win but my enemy is a sneaky son of a bitch and I have to keep my shields up, this can make me tough to be around sometimes and often a prickly old so and so.

Tough reality check for those of you living with someone with an addiction, you will never get it, I know that sucks but it is true, you will be able to support and help in many ways but an intimate and honest understanding of addiction is not one of them. You'll never know what it is like to have dreams so vivid you wake up hungover, how a smell can be so pungent that it rocks your whole day, week or month, how you can walk through a packed bar and be fine but a Christmas beer advert can make you freeze, a million little things can ruin your life and only 1 thing keeps you on the right path. Faith.

I combat this darkness with light and vigilance that I luckily use to win the fight, so far, and when I need some support, I have friends and family who help. The support you can gain from other people is astounding, I once watched a video of a group of people push a train off a person. Sometimes it feels like a train is sat on top of me and I am lucky enough to have people help me push it off. That is the thing about sobriety sometimes it feels like a train, a massive immovable object but nothing can't be overcome.

I will always be a little bit sad, a little bit scared and a little bit angry, this helps me maintain focus. I have the strength; I promise that you do to. Remember the support you need exists so just ask. Also don't put off tomorrow what can be done today and saving your own life is somewhat urgent.

## 5. Poem about alcohol 2- I might have a problem

Being an alcoholic has a few interesting side effects, I have a rather sensitive sense of smell, my tastebuds are amazing, and I always know what people are drinking around a table.

Another one is a little more infuriating, if you are out for a while with a group of friends then one of them (let's call him Keith) will tell you a story, that in itself is fine. However, an hour later Keith will tell me the same story again this time with more embellishments and fun bits...an hour after that, we get an R-rated adult only version by the end of the evening Bob saved the maiden from the castle, fought the ninjas and snapped his fingers to take out Thanos. When you are hammered you don't mind that because your pissedness (real word) is in line with the ever-increasing story. When you are sober you realize it is difficult not to think of Keith as a knob.

Another frustrating little thing is that once a drunk person gets a little Dutch courage, they feel like sharing a lot especially with an alcoholic. Having "I might have a drinking problem" sobbed at me is always fun...it is like we are the ghost of Christmas future, and we can save them. I will always talk about my sobriety with someone, I am not ashamed of it. I am ashamed of some of the things I did when drunk but my sobriety is something I am proud of.

Feel free to talk with us if you think our experiences can help you but we are not the experts, we are not fixed ourselves, we are aware how scary addiction is. So, wait until you are sober to call someone up, send them a message and have a chat.

# 6. Poem about Letch- Just havin' a laugh

My attitude to the issues women face has most certainly changed since becoming a dad to a little girl, in fact when I think on my past, at times I probably was the issue that women face.

I am a son of a proud matriarch (my dad was often away with the army), she has 4 sisters, I have an awesome big sister, loads of female cousins, Husband to an incredible wife, I work with some incredible female teachers and have taught some inspiring young ladies. Through the years I have heard them all tell me of a time when they have felt "uncomfortable" and even worse they have all laughed it off because it is normal. Normal...NORMAL, how can that be acceptable? That we live in a world where 51% of the world just expects to be harassed. This poem will hopefully show men what their daughters, wives and mums face, if they realize it is not acceptable maybe they will call it out in others, and we can cap it at the source. Of course, not all men are going to attack but I heard a great analogy once not every wasp will sting you but to not be stung you have to act as if they will.

Unfortunately, that is the world that our young ladies exist in so be the solution today, call it out, don't do it, stop being the problem in the past be the solution in the future. So, let's use the words of an incredibly strong woman Emily Pankhurst, "Let's incite this meeting to rebellion." Gentlemen drop the stereotypes and become the men our wives, mothers and daughters deserve

## 7. Poem about Racism- The But racist

As I have said before I am a Royal flush (straight, white, male, over 40) so what right do I have to write about racism. It is a question I asked, debated and discussed at length, was I right to write it? I think yes, I am right to write it, I got a lot of people to read it and my favourite comment was from a student who said, "I didn't know that someone that looked like you could write like that".

There is another reason that I wrote it, my best friend was in a pub and someone was joking and laughing, everyone in that pub looked the same, no one in the immediate vicinity would be offended but that didn't make it right. My friend called them out on it, not aggressively, he didn't knock them out he just told them it was racist. Now the person he told I know, and their reaction was massive they shouted they argued they even said it's hanging around with people like me that had made him "soft". My friend rang me, he was perturbed he didn't want to upset anyone, and didn't deserve to be spoken to in such a way but he knew he had to call it out, he told me what the other person had said, and he waited...if he was in front of me, I would have hugged him I was so proud of him.

It is up to us to change it, all of us, we need to stop it and we need to stop it now.

Saying "I'm not racist" and "All lives matter", of course they bloody do, but we don't have to talk about pigeons when it is the tigers being hunted.

## 8. Poem about Teachers 1- 8 weeks holiday
## 9. Poem about Teachers 2 - Every day is a school day

I am not writing 300 words about why I wrote these, teachers are not respected enough, not paid enough and not loved enough. These poems should improve that understanding and that is all you are getting regarding thoughts

## 10. Poem about Today- The unfair Sea

This has been the worst week ever.

Why is this happening to me?

I am so unlucky; it is like they are out to get me.

Take a breath, people catastrophize things and understandably so. Only remembering the dangerous, bad and horrible things is an outstanding survival technique. For millions of years it worked, we will avoid that place or person if they hurt us, we won't eat those unknown berries again if they killed our friend Reuben, we won't try and put a saddle on a crocodile. However, two things need to be taken into consideration: one, what is the point in surviving if we don't get to enjoy life a little? and two, if you are in a situation where you despair about a particular thing, moment or person in your life. Do what our prehistoric ancestors would do, no, not bludgeon it to death with a club. Stop doing it, stop going there, remove yourself from the situation.

I am an optimist, I haven't always been but I try to be one now, why?...It's better. However, my wife is a pessimist she hopes for the best and prepares for the worst. As a team it means we work well together she keeps my feet grounded and a level of realism in my life. I am hoping that I help her to see the light in the world. Both optimism and pessimism are dangerous things. Without the logic of pessimism, you can end up spending your whole life blindly believing that life will be fine. However, with just pessimism you never give yourself a moment to enjoy life and embrace what is right in front of you as you are too busy waiting for it to fall apart.

I got solar panels, which is awesome, however the fitters couldn't get the hooks to fit under the tiles, so they drilled 24 1-inch holes in my roof, so I have solar panels on my roof, but I also live in an inverted colander. I trusted that the fitters wouldn't screw me and apparently they have. I was absolutely spiraling and freaking out about the fact the solar panels will have to come off. That the roof will have to come off, that the liner will need to be replaced, that it will cost a fortune that I will need to sue the solar panel people and more and more and more and more and my wife told me...everything will be okay, and pointed out how cool my daughter's homework was this week and then we watched Dancing on Ice and we danced to the dances chucking my daughter about like she was a ragdoll, we all laughed a lot.

I took a breath, the problem is still there but, it is not the end of the world, no one died and it will get fixed...maybe I am rubbing off on my wife!?

A balance is required, a beautiful dance between highs and lows, peaks and troughs, dark and light...like a weird spin off Cirque Du Soleil show, where things are awesome but also terrifying. My advice is breath through the darkness and dance in the light, enjoy your life no one gets out alive.

# 11. Poem about Mums- The impossible job

I have grown up with a lot of women in my life, my mum had 4 sisters and they all had girls. My career choices: theatre, retail and education have always been female heavy (that is a quantity reference not a weight joke!) As such I have met and known a lot of mums. They all have held the weight of the world on their shoulders, they have all questioned whether they are good enough, they have all loved unconditionally and they have all realised that their kid can be a proper dickhead, sometimes.

I am going to quickly reference the two mums that I know best. Firstly, my mum tells everyone that she has bad lungs because I gave her whooping cough when I was a kid. It's probably true because she has terrible lungs, and I was always ill as a kid. I got myself into trouble a lot, famously getting bitten by a rabid dog and having to be treated for rabies. Another time my mum ignored the advice of a doctor and took me to the hospital. Good thing she did, I had chicken pox internally and was fed through tubes up my nose for a bit. She stayed by my side and even at my lowest points, she has never given up on me and always been my cheerleader. She called me sunshine as a child and I loved it, as a teenager I was embarrassed when she used that pet name but now as an adult when she sometimes utters those words, they truly fill me with joy.

The other is my wife, we were both naive and assumed that getting pregnant would be easy. It took us years but when she became pregnant, I have never seen her happier, then came 9 months of hell. She cried herself to sleep, could hardly walk and was broken by pregnancy. How she made it through that and the labor I will never know. She is stronger than I ever will be. I have taken thousands of pictures of my daughter but when I look at those taken in the first 3 months, my wife and I look like shells of ourselves. It was only after 3 months that she started to heal and believe in herself. She met other mums, made friends and helped our daughter grow and blossom. I don't say this to gain sympathy or anything like that, I say it to explain everyone's story is different, and that my wife fought tooth and nail to be a mum.

She is an incredible mum although she will never believe it. She is always worried that she isn't doing enough; that our little girl isn't getting the best experiences and chances in life. But she needn't worry she is the definition of a mama bear, she protects our girl with every fiber of her being, she goes the extra mile and nothing is too much.

I am in awe of these women and all those like them. They do an incredibly hard job and they do it as well as they can.

We love you mums.

## 12. Poem about Love- Love is spiffing

Every poet worth his salt has to have a poem about love, don't they? Mine was written slightly differently it was written in two parts.

The second incarnation and the polish came when I was best man for my little brother. He moved to the other side of the world and tricked a company into making a new job position for him just so he could be close to the woman he loves. It is remarkable what you can do when you have to. The other half was for my friend, her partner committed suicide and she was broken and hurt, and I spoke to her and she cried and she was angry but through it all she said something that amazed me. She said she was lucky, lucky to have found her person, lucky to have found true love, that it wasn't long enough but she was still lucky for the moments they had had. Through tragedy, over any distance if you are lucky enough, then love conquers us completely.

I have always been frugal with my heart. When I drank, love was something that I could use to manipulate people, a form of currency, something that I enjoyed being shown but would never give to others. I either rejected people that were good for me and tried to help or fell too hard for those that supported my toxic lifestyle. Sobriety helped so much, my feelings were truer although I did feel like a teenager again, I had always had alcohol to help with my personality and now meeting people as the real me was terrifying. I had a number of relationships but nothing stuck. Then I met my wife. The first time I met her I thought she was awesome, the second time I saw her I knew I would marry her; I have never been more certain of anything in all my life. I was hers completely and always would be. It was only meeting my wife and later when my daughter was born did I discover true love, the type of love that can make you cry just thinking about it.

Love is great, love is painful, love is fleeting, love is forever, love is everything. I truly hope that as many people as possible get to find their one, their true love, it is never too late.

# 13. Poem about my girl- Number 1 guy

My daughter was struggling with something the other day and mumbling that she couldn't do something. When she straightened her back and said, "I can't do it yet."

Before she was born, I was terrified that I wouldn't be able to do it, that I wouldn't love her enough, little did I know the untapped well of love that I had inside myself, that said I still don't think I am enough. I have been scared before but having a kid brings it to a whole new level. Even before she was born, the action started, the labor was rather sudden, and she was nearly born at home. As the paramedics were getting my screaming wife down the stairs one quietly said to the other "Make sure she comes down backwards, then I can catch the baby." What the actual fuck!

To be honest, I didn't really believe that a baby was coming until I was holding her in my arms and then everything in my life changed. It hadn't been an easy pregnancy; my wife was in pain throughout and due to a tongue tie and other elements the first few months were very hard indeed. My wife was still in pain and after multiple tests we went to a specialist. As we walked in holding my daughter, the specialist asked, "Who's baby is that?" We responded that she was ours and the specialist replied, "But you can't have children". We then found out that my wife had severe endometriosis and that our little girl was a freaking miracle. This is more evidence that my wife is an absolute machine and one of the toughest people I know. I am definitely punching above my weight.

I don't use the phrase miracle lightly. When I was younger, I never thought I would be a dad, I was too selfish, and I had no space for anyone else. Then my life changed, sobriety hit, and I met my wife. As a unit we were kick ass, but our little girl made us whole. We have our miracle, and our family unit is complete.

My little girl is an infuriating, angering, temperamental, manipulative, loving, intelligent, inquisitive, powerful, beautiful, miracle girl. Am I good dad? Am I smashing it? Absolutely not, but will I keep trying? Of course, because like she said, "I can't do it yet."

## 14. Poem about men- yellow cress

Men are rubbish at just chatting although it is hard to not be rubbish when we are brought up with, "Boys don't cry" and "Man up". These are two of my least favourite phrases. Telling a child to man up is madness when most of the men that I see are pretending and faking their way through life.

Men are terrible at talking, at venting, at crying and maybe that is because we had loads of other terrible, good-hearted men telling us to man up and not cry. So, I wrote a poem with the idea of sneaking in the concept of well-being and mindfulness behind the pretense of piss. (pretense of piss is a good name for a punk album). In itself I hope that I can highlight the challenges and issues we all face with peeing standing up but also men should talk more.

- To the people who need to talk, go and talk to someone.
- To those of you who volunteer to listen, do just that, listen, don't judge, don't compare, don't boast, just listen.
- Some of us don't want to talk because we don't need it fixed. We just want you to know what we are thinking.

I don't do it enough because I need to be strong, because I need to hold it together, no one can see the cracks. I am aware that all of those things are excuses and that I have people who love me and will listen...for now that's enough. Also, my poems help and that is a big part of why writing them works as a release, a way of venting but nothing beats chatting to a person...I will try harder.

# 15. Poem about Black dog- My dog is different

I like the imagery of the black dog; I like that it gives it weight and depth. That it is this morphing entity that sometimes can fit in your pocket whilst at other times it can swallow you whole. That is how my mental health has felt at times, a monster that can swallow me whole but at other times something I hold in my hands and show people and talk about it. When the artist (the artwork is amazing) was making the page headers she originally made the black dog a smooth Labrador looking fella, I asked her to change it. My dog is a rough and scabby looking thing that will bite your ankles when you least expect it.

I am not fit but I work with healthy people and hear about bodysmash classes, maximum lift weights and fastest laps, even the unhealthiest amongst us will proudly tell others about the crunches they attempted or the salad they had. We discuss our physical health with people even when they really, really, really, really, really don't care. People will blindly waffle about, cleanses, intermittent fasting, cupping and Bikram yoga but when asked if you are okay, we will probably say, "yeah good!"

I am not sure if it is the stiff upper lip nature of Brits or whether it is a human nature thing where we don't want to show any kind of psychological weakness. Are we afraid that people will latch onto it and use it against us, that we might scare people away, that they may look at us differently. You know what? That might be true, but your true friends care about you, they want to know you and they want to help you because you help them too.

Your dog isn't going away but the size of that unyielding beast is dependent on you and how you live with it. Share it with people, talk to people, be safe with people. So next time, don't just boast about the 17 burpees you smashed out at the weekend but talk about the fact you are in a good place and really talk if you are in a difficult place.

## 16. Poem about Cancer- Nuff said

I have a healthy disdain for death. I don't particularly fear death, but I would like to live as long as possible. Death is inevitable and as they say life is a game where no one gets out alive. But cancer isn't the same as death, it doesn't offer a level playing field it indiscriminately rains fear, evil and decimation in its wake. I have had friends taken by it, I have seen people wracked by it and I have had scares myself. As a silent, daunting unwavering ghoul, it is difficult not to be scared by it.

When my big sister was diagnosed, I was terrified, but she went to social media, and she wrote, "I will kick cancers ass!" I kind of felt bad for cancer, my sister is a force of nature, and she will rip trees asunder if it means staying alive for her family. The cost was great, but she lived, and I realized that one of the reasons she won was that she didn't bow and shiver, she hated it and beat it. I have spoken to other people who have faced cancer and they all describe it as a combatant, a living breathing thing they can face and defeat and that gives them strength and it gives those around them strength, and that is why I hold it I disdain. It isn't an overbearing all powerful specter...it is a dick.

The unfortunate thing is that regrettably in a fight, sometimes the other person wins and that is awful but we must keep fighting.

Every fight won is another life saved and another kick in the balls to cancer.

# 17. Poem about white Britishness-Mongrel Nation

I am still not sure why I wrote this, I was in a bad mood and was questioning my relationship with who I was and it was a topic that bothered me. I look like someone you don't want to meet in an alley, I have a beard a shaven head I weigh over a 100kg (240 lbs); because my brain is thinking about a million things at once, I look miserable a lot of the time and even worse when I smile. With my size and haircut, I do have a certain EDLish quality which I am not a fan of.

For example, I was on an equality spearheading panel once and it was a very diverse group of people, as you would expect. The only other white person in the group was a woman whose views were rather old fashioned for the audience. Her statements were divisive, cruel and not thought out, she was however aware enough to notice the rest of the panel were looking at her with open mouths. At which point she noticed me and said, "You know what I mean, don't you?"...Her stereotyped view of the world went so far that of course the other white person is a bigot as well; it infuriated me, how dare you tar me with that brush? Everyone looked at me and I honestly replied, "I have no idea what you are talking about."

My views are far more liberal, my grandad was gay, well he was bisexual. He loved my grandmother dearly and they raised 5 beautiful girls together. After her death he met other people that he cared for, and they happened to be male. His boyfriend was an Ethiopian prince, not sure if this is factually correct or just a pet name from my grandad. From the age of 8 when my parents went to London, my sister and I would be dropped off at my grandfather's "wine bar" in Chelsea and we would be excellently looked after. When I say this to people, they are shocked, but this was my normal. My views of the world were that anyone could love anyone, and my views of London (my countries capital), was that everyone belonged and that everyone was different. I was oblivious to the hate crimes, to all of the isms, to the bombs in the clubs in SOHO. The fact is that when my grandfather was a younger man homosexuality would have been illegal in this country. The naivety of youth and my parents need for a babysitter meant my upbringing was, in my mind, perfect.

I am older now and less naïve, but I keep those youthful opinions and hopefully pass them on to my daughter. Unfortunately, I see a lot more hate, wider access and social media means that spewing rancid hatred is available 24 hours a day, seven days a week, people arguing and hating each other for the most ridiculous reasons. People have confused freedom of speech with an excuse to be a dick, in fact not just a dick a justified dick with righteousness on their side. The problem with a lot of these justified dicks is that it isn't righteousness next to them, just a couple of nuts!

I am proud to be British and be part of the smorgasbord that is this united country but why dirty and muddy this awesome thing by thinking your Britishness means more than someone else's. So, what if you were born here and love Britain? Lots of other people became who they really are here or literally had their lives saved by being here...how can you have more love for your country than that person? Yes, some people hate this country and that is a discussion for another book but for now just realize the ridiculousness of arguing that you love something more than someone else.

Embrace Britishness, not mauve, turquoise, or magenta. Britishness just Britishness

## 18. Poem about Annoyance- Legitimate slowness

Alanis Morisette ruined Ironic for everyone, I can never work out if something is Ironic or frustrating and if it is frustrating it annoys me. So, I am not sure if this is ironic or merely annoyance, but I cannot finish this blurb. I am wondering whether it is because I am like the hulk but instead of always angry, I am always peeved, frustrated, annoyed.

I am British and middle aged and I live in the country and therefore I have no massive issues in my life. My life is good: beautiful wife, awesome daughter, a job that I don't hate. Which obviously means I have to fill my days with being frustrated with stuff that most people wouldn't even waste a moment with.

The rest of these poems are linked to a moment, an emotion, a specific subject matter but this is proper meandering, ramblings of an old man. It is also a poem without end, I have already composed about 4 more verses, and I cannot see an end any time soon. As long as the world continues to turn, it will persist on throwing things into my orbit to frustrate me and to write about them. Because I think it is okay to be annoyed by things, to have things tick you off, as long as you let it pass and don't go all Michael Douglas in Breaking Point or road rage on the street.

I am happy for you to continue to overcook vegetables, park badly, not say please and thank you, put too many advert breaks in. That will allow me to keep on sweating the small stuff and just like Alanis, writing fun, sometimes confusing, little ditties.

# 19. Poem about age- Rolling stone
# 20. Poem about Pressure- Saggy bits and flappy bits

How is it possible that we are still worrying about the stuff that we were worrying about when we were kids and teenagers, it is literally the same old shit on a different day.

I thought that I got to get fat and bald, that I didn't have to care what people thought or what I looked like; instead I am surrounded by images of octogenarians doing calisthenics on the side of mountains as the sunsets behind them. They are doing that whilst I have special pants so my thighs don't rub and, the best invention I have found in the last few years is stretchy jeans. I make noises as I get up and incredibly a different part of me hurts every day just to keep me guessing. I take vitamins and supplements and do some basic exercise, but everything is so dang hard.

This insta world continues to strip back the world to its basic form, it is like the cool kids from school, instead of smoking and kissing by the bike sheds, are now getting stuff for free and telling us we should buy it whilst desperately trying to get you to follow or watch them. We seem so happy to mock teenagers and the "youth of today" as they blindly follow influencers and the latest craze but surely, we are just the same even with our advanced years and wisdom we take supplements, we go to boxercise, we eat kale, we follow our own influencers and read books not watch Tik Toks.

What is best:
- ranting about teenagers and berating them for being younger than us?
- whining after a forgotten youth that we believe was better than it probably was?
- grow up disgracefully, middle finger raised to society, getting hammered, tattooed, and giddy at every opportunity?
- grow up as our parents did, with high waisted trousers, looking old, driving old, being like properly old?

I guess there is no right way of doing it so maybe don't do it some other way. Just do it your own way but let's follow some rules.

1. You do you.
2. Your feeling better about getting old shouldn't be at the expense of someone

else.

3. Don't hurt other people.

4. Don't hurt yourself.

5. Accept it, it happens to us all.

6. Do not regret the things you do, regret the things you didn't do.

7. Everyone gets a second chance.

8. Most of all try not to stress about stuff. Easier said than done but try.

# 21. Poem about Manly men- Keeping it up

I assume you have read the poem and realize that the poem is not about erections, that was just me going all Carry on Film with the title.

I am shocking at DIY, that is probably unfair I am getting better through necessity. However, I am still pretty terrible at it, also DIY is changing. As a kid I was brought up under the illusion that putting up a shelf or maybe some flatpack furniture was doing it yourself. That was the benchmark that existed everything else would be a trade person's job. Now I live in a world where people say, "Oh I did some DIY at the weekend...I re roofed my house!" That is not fucking DIY. That is an alternate career as a bloody roofer. I am all smug because I put a corner shelf in, even cutting gaps for the pipes and these "DIYers" are boarding and paneling the loft or relaying a drive or fitting new carpets.

Some of this rant is straight up jealousy. I wish I could be better with my hands. I can plan, design, envision but not create, and that does frustrate me. I would like to be able to build, make and create to make what is in my head become real. To save money and not having to pay full price; for my daughter to learn these things from me. But I can't and she won't.

With age comes wisdom and wisdom (and my wife!) tells me that I do not have to be brilliant at everything.That my skills don't have to mean a mastery of carpentry, plumbing and metal work. I am allowed to be good at other things. I am very very good at getting 3 quotes and then picking the middle one and getting that professional to do an excellent job.

I suppose the takeaways are that everyone is good at different things, and that I don't have to be good at everything, and that I shouldn't be jealous but the main one is that without the rubbish DIYers like me these people would be out of work.

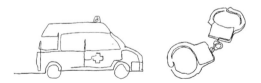

## 22. Poem about Violence 1- Washed in the rain
## 23. Poem about Violence 2- Pushing buttons

This incident broke me, it really did. It affected me physically, psychologically, it invaded my work and social life and pushed me so incredibly close to the brink it would have been easier to fall than to stay standing. It was only through talking to people, the understanding of my friends and my incredible wife that I stayed on my path. In retrospect there are two things that really stand out from this incident, the different types of bystanders and the importance of talking.

As I stated in the poem, I was not the one who was attacked. I was a witness, I didn't stand by, I tried to help, to offer advice, apply pressure, to raise legs. I once heard a statement regarding atrocities that no matter how bad it is and how many people are running away or fleeing there will always be those that run towards incidents, to help where they can. The attack I saw only stopped before someone was killed because members of the public gathered together and scared the attacker away. The victim only lived because people with training learnt, mostly, from TV, valiantly tried to hold them together, and the victim only didn't succumb because an off-duty doctor stepped up. These people are heroes. However, there were other onlookers... When I was looking for synonyms of onlooker one word popped up to describe these people "sightseers". When the incident first happened, I ran to find a first aid kit from anywhere and saw a large group of people approaching from a car show room. They had been attracted by the noise, not enough to approach when it was loud and scary but now it is quieter, maybe there will be gossip. I asked if they had a first aid kit, they said no. As I rushed back with a scarf from my boot to use as a bandage I suggested not to go up as the scene was disgusting, they ignored me, some lit cigarettes and vaped as they watched, others took pictures. The two sides of society brought together over the body of a man ripped apart by hate. In this moment I decided two things, one I will always run towards and two I will never ever ever buy that brand of car.

Talking to people, I have used therapy a few times before and have been an on and off visitor to group therapy with AA for years, but on this occasion the need to chat was overwhelming. The psychological effects were immediate and started with nightmares straight away. I would see the attack but the person being hurt would change to people I know. Then I started having waking dreams I would be teaching a class and almost have an outer body experience, reliving the attack and then completely losing where I was or what I was doing. The waking dreams became very intense, hurtling my subconscious into a scene it didn't want to be in with such force I felt vertigo. I am blessed that several of my confidants in life are very good listeners and have excellent advice. No one could fix the issue I just needed people to listen, to empathise, to be there...and they were.

I will never forget what happened and what I saw, it will stay with me forever. I hope that I will learn from the experience and hopefully become better because of it. Hatred will always exist, but we can banish the darkness with light, with doing what's right, with talking and with listening.

## 24. Poem about Unicorns- Their mojo doesn't fail

After writing the two poems about violence I was in a funk. I had tainted my poetry and was worried that I wouldn't be able to regain the balance I had before. I always tried to write with a balance of opinion, fact, and humour, and with violence the topic didn't allow for humour. I turned back to my original muse my girl. She never fails to make me feel better, she is rather astute when it comes to how people feel which makes her a great manipulator but also excellent at checking you are okay. She gives the best hugs and always wants to play. She is passionate about things and is always up for a chat.

So, I stopped trying to write for a bit and played more and after many rambling, meandering, nonsense adventures I started smiling and laughing more and I realized that I was trying too hard. I started writing again, I started a thousand poems but still couldn't find a hook a handle a topic that would flow easily. And as my daughter is telling me what to do most of the times, I asked her what to write about and that is how I ended up writing about unicorns.

I read a post that stated when you look at cartoon unicorns they are all drawn the same way. They all have closed eyes to make them look subdued and demure to encourage young girls to also be demure and subdued. Well that shit ain't working on my little girl. She is all about the warrior unicorn, a weapon wielding, rainbow tailed, equine superhorse. The unicorn in her mind is a buddy, a friend in arms that will accompany her into battles or on adventures.

I will always love unicorns, The national animal of Scotland (it's true look it up!) is awesome. It's difficult not to love it. My little girl and unicorns got my mojo back and allowed me to see the light in the world.

## 25. Poem about New parents- Avalanche of crap

Congratulations you are a new parent, this is the best thing that has ever happened to you. The rewards are astronomical, you have witnessed and will witness more miracles.

Now that is out the way, may I say you will never be good enough!

This is the hardest job in the world it is impossible, and hard, and trying, and painful, and awful but still the human race has kids, but that is because it is wonderful, and beautiful, and incredible, and perfect and everything.

The moment that you think you have something nailed the goalposts shift and the initial issue either disappears or morphs into some other seemingly terrifying monster. My main example of this is the absolute naivety that I approached teething. I assumed a couple of months, but no it lasts years and the possible side effects are insane:

- their gum is sore and red where the tooth is coming through.
- they have a mild temperature of less than 38C.
- they have 1 flushed cheek.
- they have a rash on their face.
- they're rubbing their ear.
- they're dribbling more than usual.
- they're gnawing and chewing on things a lot.
- they're more fretful than usual.
- they're not sleeping very well.
- They may have diarrhoea.

What the actual fuck? These are also the symptoms of a hangover, eating an extra hot curry, or turning into a werewolf...although in all honesty only one of these scenarios is likely with a small child.

These lists are helpful, and I appreciate it, but I typed teething symptoms into Google, and I got 8,000,080 results in 0.56 seconds. In the darkest despair of the middle of the night, and as I trawled through all 8 million results pretty much everything in the world is a chuffing symptom of teething ...so I buckled in for the ride and prayed that everyone gets some sleep. You know what? In the morning everything was fine, my daughter giggled and laughed and reached for me and my wife, and the night from hell evaporated into the back of my mind.

I really wanted to write something that showed that seesaw of despair to delight and hopefully highlight, that sometimes the worst of times gives way to the best of times. That every single one of us thinks we can't do it but when we try our best, we make it through and end up in a place that makes it all feel like a distant memory.

# The last word.

That's it. I am spent. Stick a fork in me, I am done. These bits at the end have killed me but let me know what you think on Instagram, thebeardybloke110 and that I will be releasing new content on the 27th of every month.

I hope that you liked the book and be aware I have more coming....well that's if people liked this one that is, and if some very sensible publisher has snapped me up as the next big thing in poetry.

Not sure the next big thing in poetry is an actual thing.